D0955770

The
Old-Time
Bicycle Book

The Old-Time Bicycle Book

By Lynn Lee Monroe/ pictures by George Overlie

Carolrhoda Books · Minneapolis, Minnesota

LIBRARY OF CONGRESS CATALOGING IN PUBLICATION DATA

Monroe, Lynn Lee.
The old-time bicycle book.

(On my own books)
SUMMARY: Describes the invention of the bicycle and
traces its development from the Hobby Horse, the Ariel, and
other early models to today's multispeed vehicles.

1. Bicycles and tricycles — History — Juvenile literature.
[1. Bicycles and bicycling — History] I. Overlie, George. II. Title.

TL410.M65   629.22'72'09   79-52422
ISBN 0-87614-110-6 lib. bdg.

1 2 3 4 5 6 7 8 9 10 85 84 83 82 81 80 79

Not so long ago, people didn't have cars.

They didn't have buses.

They didn't even have bicycles.

When they went some place, they walked.

Or they rode a horse.

Or they rode in something
a horse could pull.

But horses got hungry.

They got tired.

People wished they had something better.

Some people did more than wish.

They invented.

Inventions do not happen all at once.

The first car didn't look
like cars today.

And the first bike didn't look
like bikes today.

This is the story of
the invention of the bicycle.
It took many years.
And there were many different
kinds of bikes before
the bike we have today was invented.

The very first bike

was called a Hobby Horse.

It looked like a toy horse on wheels.

Sometimes it looked like a lion.

The Hobby Horse didn't have pedals.

People pushed it with their feet.

The front wheel could not turn.

So they could only go straight.

But they could go faster

than they could go on foot.

Forester's Bicycle
1817

Twenty-six years later

people still rode Hobby Horses.

But one man wanted something better.

His job was to take care of a forest.

He was called a forester.

The forest was very large.

It took a long time

just to walk through it.

The forester wanted a bike.

Then he could do his job much faster.

But the paths through the forest

were not straight.

He needed a bike

that could turn corners.

So he invented one.

He made a front wheel that could turn.

He added handlebars.

He could steer it!

The forester was proud of his bike.

Sometimes he rode it to town.

At first people laughed.

But before long they wanted bikes too.

Soon many rich young men
were riding them.
These men were called Dandies.
So the bikes they rode
were called Dandy Horses.

Ladies' Dandy Horse
1818

Women wanted bikes too.

But they could not ride Dandy Horses.

Their long dresses got in the way.

So the Ladies' Dandy Horse was made.

The bar between the wheels was lower.

And there was a better seat.

But there were still problems

with the Dandy Horse.

It was made of wood and iron.

So it was very heavy.

People pushed it with their feet.

That was hard work.

And their shoes wore out quickly.

Most people thought
the riders looked silly.

They made fun of them.

Soon no one wanted
to ride Dandy Horses any more.

First Pedaled Bicycle

1839

No one dreamed that a person

could sit on two wheels

without touching his feet

to the ground.

Then a man in Scotland had an idea.

In 1839 he invented pedals.

Now he could go faster.

And his feet never touched the ground.

The man learned many tricks.

He loved to show off.

But no one else

wanted to ride his bike.

"He must know magic," they said.

"That is what keeps him

from falling off."

In the whole world he was the only one
to ride a bike with pedals.
Then he stopped riding.
And no one remembered his invention.
Pedals had to be invented
all over again!

Boneshaker *1861*

Of course, they were.

But it happened 22 years later!

A man in France

was fixing an old Hobby Horse.

There must be a better way, he thought.

There was. And he found it.

He was the second inventor of pedals.

But his bike was made

of wood and iron too.

So were its wheels.

What a bumpy ride!

People called his bike the Boneshaker!

One day an American
was riding his Boneshaker.
Bump! Bump! Bump!
This can not be good for me, he thought.
Suddenly he had an idea.
Why not put rubber tires on the wheels?
He did. And it worked!

Ariel

1870

But Boneshakers were still heavy.

Rubber tires didn't help that.

A man in England wanted a lighter bike.

He made one out of metal and rubber.

He named it the Ariel.

It had a high front wheel.

That made the bike go faster.

He put the seat over the front wheel.

That made it easier to pedal.

But it made the seat hard to get to.

People didn't mind, though.

Soon many men, not just the rich,

were riding the new bike.

Ordinary people rode it.

So they began to call it the Ordinary.

Racing Ordinary
1879

Some people wanted to go even faster.

So they made the front wheel higher.

They called their bike

the Racing Ordinary.

Riders still sat over the front wheel.

That was dangerous

when they hit a bump.

Then they would fly
over the handlebars.
They hit the road head first!
But that didn't bother racers.
They made the front wheel
higher and higher and higher.
It got harder and harder
to climb up to the seat.
Soon only the very tallest men
could race the Ordinary.

For the Timid
1876

One boy in England felt badly.

He wanted to ride a bike.

But he could not climb up to the seat

of an Ordinary.

So he invented a new bike.

Timid means afraid.

The For the Timid was a bike

for people afraid to ride the Ordinary.

It had a small front wheel.

It had a large back wheel.

The rider sat in between.

Falling was not frightening.

Your feet were close to the ground.

Now the boy could ride a bike.

But no one else wanted to.

Most people were still afraid.

Tricycle

1877

Some of those people

tried riding tricycles.

Tricycles got very popular.

This is why.

One day the Queen of England

was riding in her coach.

A young woman was riding her tricycle

in front of the coach.

She saw the coach coming.

She had to get out of the way.

So she pedaled as fast as she could.

Soon she was out of sight.

The queen thought this was wonderful.

She found out who the girl was.

Then she invited the girl to the palace.

Soon all the princes and princesses
were riding tricycles.

Crocodile
1879

The boy who invented his own bike
was still inventing.

This time he made a chain and sprocket
to turn the wheels.

Before this, pedals had to be attached
to one of the wheels.

For every time you turned the pedals,
the wheel only went around once!

The chain and sprocket
made it much easier to pedal.
And people could go faster.
But no one wanted to try it.
People just laughed at this bike.
They called it the Crocodile.

American Star
1880

Another bike was being invented
in America.
It was called the American Star.
It looked like a backwards Ordinary.
It had a large wheel in the back.
It had a small wheel up front.

Riders sat over the back wheel.
This put more weight at the back
than at the front.
Now when riders hit bumps,
they fell off the back.
No one liked this bike much either.

Safety Bicycle
1885

Finally there was a bike people liked.

It was called the Safety Bike.

It was light. It was safe.

It was easy to ride.

Riders didn't fall off the front.

They didn't fall off the back.

They could raise and lower the seat.

So it didn't matter if they were short.

There was a Safety Bike for women too.

The bar between its wheels was lower.

So women's dresses

didn't get in the way.

Some women even wore pants.

These pants were called bloomers.

They made bike riding even easier.

Now more and more people
were riding bikes.
More and more people
were inventing bikes too.
Some of those people had a new idea.
What if two people could ride
the same bike, they thought.
What fun that would be!

Club Convertible
1886

One bicycle for two

was the Club Convertible.

It had four wheels.

There were two high wheels

in the middle.

There was a little wheel up front.

There was a little wheel in the back.

Riders sat between the two high wheels.

Another bicycle for two

had three wheels.

It was called the Sociable.

The bicycle for two was very popular.

There was even a song about it.

Soon bicycles were made for three
or four or five or even more.
One bicycle was made for ten!

Monocycle
1869

Everyone wanted to invent a bike.

Some were very funny.

One was the Monocycle.

Riders sat in the middle

of a very large wheel.

They leaned to the side to turn corners.

They leaned back to stop.

The big wheel turned around them.

French Giraffe
1890s

There were bikes with one wheel.

There were bikes with two wheels

side by side.

But perhaps the funniest bike of all

was the French Giraffe.

Circus people rode this bike.

There are stories of people

riding it across tightropes!

But soon people stopped
inventing bikes.

A new invention had come—the car.

People got very excited about the car.

They forgot about bicycles.

No one wanted to invent a new bike.

They just wanted to invent cars.

For 50 years no one invented a bike.

Then a man in England did.

His bike had little wheels.

It had fancy trim.

It had fenders.

At first no factory wanted to make it.

"Who would buy it?" they asked.

Finally one factory took a chance.

Then children saw it.

They loved it.

Parents began to buy bikes
for their children.

And bicycles began
to get popular again.

Today biking is more popular than ever.

And not just with children!

It's popular with grown-ups too.

Bikes don't crowd the streets.

They don't pollute the air.

They don't make a lot of noise.

But best of all,

biking is a lot of fun.